I'M STILL HERE

The story of a survivor

Noah Nash

For permission requests, visit www.noahnashauthor.com.
Please write to the author, addressed
"Attention: Permissions Coordinator."

First printing, 2024.
Copyright © 2024 Noah Nash.
ISBN: 979-8-218-40453-6
eBook ISBN: 979-8-218-40454-3

Library of Congress Cataloging-in-Publication Data
is available upon request.

The events in this book are memories from the author's perspective.
All names have been changed to protect
the identities of those involved.

Cover design by Julia Moore. Photograph by Julia Moore.
Printed in the United States of America.

Dedicated to all survivors of gun violence.

And to my dogs, who keep me safe.

Preface

Five years ago, I sat alone in a friend's garage, where it was 90 degrees on a hotter than average day in August. I was wearing a worn-out wife-beater tank top and ratty old jeans, and I was emotionally at my lowest point in years. I sat on the hard cement floor, my back against a disgusting old couch that I had been forced to sleep on for a few days.

I hung my head, totally dejected, as I contemplated what seemed to be my only option. As my dogs looked on, I swallowed a bottle of pills and waited. I waited for my eyes to get blurry before I lost consciousness. I waited for an end to my troubles. I had been living on the streets and in my car, with two dogs, in sweltering heat for weeks, and I knew I could not go on like this.

As I sat there, I felt my mind go back and forth between the present and the past, and I felt the need to reach out one last time, to someone who had helped me. I wrote to a person who had donated to my GoFundMe two years earlier when I was featured in an online article about survivors of mass shootings.

At the time, I used the money to care for my dogs, and I also intended to go back to college. For some reason, I felt the need to find this person online and say, '*thank you*,' as I had not done so at the time. It was something I just felt I needed to do.

I never expected to hear back from this person, but I did. After some text messages were exchanged, this person remarked on my ability to express myself in writing and suggested that I write a book about my life. I said that I was already keeping journals, and that I tend to either write or paint when I need to get out of my head. That was the moment that this project was born.

I don't know how we did it, in spite of all the chaos that the world has seen in these last few years, but we got it done. So many people talk about writing a book, but I have actually done it. It meant digging into my past and reliving some horrible moments, and I couldn't have done it without the support of this person. Someone once said that it only takes one person to believe in you, and I consider myself lucky to have one very special person who does.

Through perseverance and some hard-headed optimism, I am still here. I have gotten to a place where the memories of the trauma do not control me, and I can go to work and live my life without being constantly bombarded by those images. I still feel safest when I am in my home, with my dogs. But while life still presents its challenges, writing this book has helped me to leave the past in the past. I would recommend writing or journaling to any survivors out there, and I look forward to what happens next.

May 20, 1998: Nothing to Worry About

It was a Spring morning, and I woke up and got everything ready to start a typical day as a high school freshman at Thurston High School in Springfield, Oregon. All my morning chores done, I was dressed and ready to go to school. My father, a county sheriff who was separated from my mother, picked me up at 7:25 a.m.

I didn't see him as much as I'd like, but he had just started picking me up in the morning and dropping me off at school. When he could, he'd take me out to lunch. Every once in a while, when he had time, he would pick me up from school and take me home. These were the only times I saw my father during the first year of my parents' separation after he asked my mother for a divorce.

I was 14 at the time. My brother was 17. I always enjoyed my time with my dad, even though I always knew it was going to be short. But at least I got to see him. I knew my dad was going to be picking me up every morning because the gym was just down the street from school, and he was always there for his 8 a.m. workout.

I found school challenging. I'm not a standard learner,

and at the time that wasn't something schools were good at accommodating. I really only enjoyed Science, PE, and my two band classes: Jazz Ensemble and Wind Ensemble. I did not care for much more than those classes, as I had no interest in Language Arts, and I disliked Math intensely. I felt as if the teachers taught the way they wanted to instead of teaching the way some of us learned. I often felt left out in the cold and open to failure. We had a more flexible schedule then some high schools, so I always made sure I had double lunch and I often skipped classes I hated. That day, I went to the music room to grab my Tenor Saxophone and practice.

I generally avoided the crowds in the hallway…and tests and public speaking. I felt very out of place in school. I always felt misunderstood, unable to keep up with certain classes. I had trouble expressing my feelings and with making and keeping friends. Just communicating could be difficult. I often felt like I was in the wrong place at the wrong time.

After lunch, I had science class, and I would leave the music room and walk down the hallway through the crowds. No one was ever really mean or rude as my family was well known throughout the school district, and my father was with the Sheriff's Office. Also, our community was small, and all of my peers were raised together at the same schools from Kindergarten through High School.

Walking from the music room to my science class on the other side of school, I walked by the lockers and there were four cops, a fellow student, and all the office administrators. The student was being put into handcuffs and one of the cops was holding a pistol, which I figured belonged to the student being led away.

I'm not sure we could be considered good friends, but we were friendly and lived near each other. I was not too surprised he had brought a pistol to school, knowing how we were raised and where we lived. While parts of Oregon are very liberal, there are large pockets of the state that are pretty conservative…and even many liberals here own guns. Many of the students at my school hunted and enjoyed target practice so I didn't think too much of it at this point. The staff and officers walked him away. The student had his head down low, not making eye contact, and tears were streaming down his face. It was a very awkward silence, but all of us students were told to carry on and that there was nothing to worry about.

I went to science class not thinking much of the situation at all. Class ended and I went back to the music room to finish out my day, and then went to be picked up by my dad in front of the school and I went home.

It was later that night when I received a phone call from the kid who had been arrested. He didn't say much. I now remember wondering what was up with the Romeo and Juliet music playing in the background. I tried convincing him to let me come up and visit as his parents and my parents worked closely together; my mother worked at the school district and his parents were teachers. He lived just up the river from us.

Usually, no matter how much trouble my friend got into, I was allowed to come over, even if it meant we were not allowed to leave his house. The student said his parents were acting differently about this situation and no one was allowed to come see him. I found out later that he had stolen his father's gun earlier that day and had brought it to school. I knew that he was probably expelled or was going to be, and that he was looking at some serious consequences as his family was very involved in the school district, and the community.

But that night, it didn't seem like a big deal to me. I was sorry for the guy but didn't think much of it beyond that. I went about my night, just doing the usual things like having dinner with my mom and brother, avoiding my homework, enjoying some television...it was Wednesday, and I always watched Beverly Hills 90210. We were allowed to stay up later than usual to watch the show as a family. Afterwards, I did my nighttime routine and crawled into bed with not a single thought in my mind except that I did not want to go to school the following day. I closed my eyes and went to sleep.

The next morning, I opened my eyes at 6:00 a.m. on a crisp, sunny, Spring morning with the birds chirping, the neighbor's dog barking, the train in the distance going around the mountains, and my mother yelling at me to get out of bed. I was blissfully unaware that I had more to worry about than how to avoid math.

Morning, May 21, 1998: Direct Hit

I was hiding out in the band room. I hadn't heard any gun shots for a while when someone banged on the door. I was afraid it was the shooter at first, so I was hesitant to open the door. When I did, a girl ran in. She didn't even know she was shot. Blood was running down her leg, she was screaming.

I'd never seen that much blood. I freaked out and ran from the band room into the back of the adjacent uniform room and hid in between all the marching band uniforms. I waited for a while and then, after what felt like an eternity, the banging on the door began again. I didn't know what to do until I heard my dad's voice. That's when I knew it was safe to step out. It was less than an hour after the shooting, and my dad had guessed where I'd be. But after hearing bullets and the screams of my fellow students during the shooting, that hour of waiting was a horror that is seared into my memory — indelibly and forever.

I remember just falling into my father's arms. I didn't know what to feel. I didn't know what to say. Or what to do. I remember him holding me tight and telling me everything was going to be okay. We embraced for a minute or so and he said, "Come on, son, I need to take you to your mom at work." As my father led me out of the band room into the hallway and I opened the door, I remember getting yelled at and told not to step there by someone. When I looked down, it was a puddle of blood from a student's head-wound. I walked down that dark hallway towards the courtyard. There was blood everywhere, backpacks just laying where people had dropped them. And so little sound; just a cold, silent feeling that I had never felt before. There were police all over, and we passed several as we walked into the courtyard.

My father held me close and told me not to look in the cafeteria. But of course, I did. I will never forget the feeling I had in my stomach as we walked past. Dread. Horror. Fear. Emptiness. Dad and I walked out to the front of the school past the police who were surrounding the building. I could see students embracing other students. Embracing their parents. We kept walking, and as I continued, I saw in the distance all the news media trucks starting to show up, lining the streets in front of the building.

I was so angry that somehow this was a news story. I flipped the news reporters off because I really didn't want my face to be on the front of a newspaper or on a nationwide news media outlet. I got in my dad's Toyota truck and just sat there. My father said nothing to me except that he missed me, and he loved me. "I love you, too," I replied. Sitting there, my head was spinning. I was having these random thoughts of the images I had just seen. Every movement startled me. Every sound made me jump. I thought the whole world was out to get me, and that is where my fragile emotional state of mind started to show its true colors, after the trauma that had just occurred. It was a blank stare and a shock and awe kind of moment. I was so tired and upset. I didn't know how to act. I didn't know what to say to my dad. As we pulled into the parking lot of the school district office, I saw my mom. She was crying. She had not seen my father except in passing since the divorce, so it was awkward and awful. My mom and dad shook hands.

This was the last time I was together with them both. I embraced my mom, who in return gave me a small pat on the back. My father gave me a bear hug and did not loosen up for at least a minute. I looked him in the eye and said, "Thank you." I said again, "I love you, Dad." He turned around and got back in his truck. My mom and I waved at him but didn't realize that this would be a moment that marked another historic point in my life, all in one day, for us all. I was in shock, traumatized, and my dad got me to a safe place. Little did any of us know, this would be the last time I saw him alive.

People talk about having a terrible year. They mean so many things by that. To say that 1998 was a tough year for me, is a huge understatement. So much damage, so much blood, so much loss. It was the year that changed me forever. Sometimes it still seems unbelievable that I survived it all, and that I've survived to see the anniversary of this fateful day come and go many times over. But somehow, I lived to tell the tale.

May 21, 1998: Nightmares and Night Terrors

Directly after going through the tragedy of the shooting at my high school, I had no idea what was ahead. That night, when I finally managed to sleep, was the first time I ever experienced a night terror. Before the tragedy, I had always slept well and had been able to wake up with no fear for the day.

I went to sleep the night of the tragedy, and I did not realize that from that moment forward, I would never sleep the same again. I had never experienced a night terror before, but was I ever in for a rude awakening, so to speak. I went from sleeping soundly for years to all of a sudden being woken up by visions of chaos and terror, and horrible past scenes replaying in my dreams.

I remember the first night and the intensity of that first terror. I woke up shaking, tears in my eyes, sweat dripping from my forehead. I remember yelling for help, and I wasn't sure why. I finally snapped out of it and realized when I fully woke up that I was dreaming that I was still in the school, even though in the dream it was later in the evening. I felt like I could not escape this nightmare. I was confused and had no idea what to think, except that I did not want to close my eyes ever again, out of fear that I would hear the gunshots or my peers at school screaming.

I didn't dare go back to sleep, so I stayed up the rest of the night. There was no school the next day, but I went to a memorial site in front of the school where people had started to put flowers and notes to us from other schools and from other people around the world and from the community. What was once a fence that was supposed to keep us students safe had been turned into a memorial for all of us who had suffered from this tragedy. News media trucks were everywhere, from local news to CNN.

We no longer had privacy as a school. We had to park several blocks down the street and walk in, since there was no way to drive directly up to the school anymore. Walking past each student and parent was intense for me; I could feel their energy, and it was a sad and gloomy feeling. Seeing other peers embracing one another, there was no more separation between the different classes or the people. It was the first time that I saw our community stand as one. Even if it took a tragedy such as this, it's good to know that when it comes down to it, we can and will stand together.

The second night was even more intense because now I was afraid that I was going to have that same nightmare and I felt a sense of dread about going to sleep. Unfortunately, this troubled sleep was to become a long-lasting companion from that day. One I still deal with today.

If I fall asleep, I don't stay asleep for long—maybe a few hours—then I wake up and even if it's the middle of the night, I have to find a way to get out of my head. Sometimes I do abstract paintings, sometimes I write, sometimes I clean obsessively, trying to scrub the memories from my mind. I can't worry about how much sleep I've lost over the years. It's just part of dealing with what happened to me.

It's a Cul-de-Sac Life

G rowing up in the hills and suburbs of Springfield, Oregon, it was quiet, secluded, and the stars were bright at night. My entire childhood was pretty secluded...just the way I like it. I didn't have many friends, and I didn't really enjoy the company of others. Two houses down, there were two older girls who I would visit. They would use me as their test subject for makeup. I always enjoyed myself. Besides that, it was me, my family, and my grandparents right next door in the other side of the duplex we lived in.

As time went on, the Thurston Hills became more popular for investing in property and the forest was slowly but surely taken over by houses. Society had started to become a part of our lives. I hated it. I used to go around and throw rocks into all the windows of the brand-new houses—granted, I was only 13 and I was annoyed at having to listen to the noisy work trucks every morning when all I used to hear was the sound of the birds and the train in the morning coming around the mountain.

One time, I was outside playing basketball on the street and this family came walking by with an enormous black dog named Grizzly. He was huge. I remember the parents stopping me and asking how I liked the area and how the schools were and just making small talk. I was quickly done with talking to them, but then they said they had two sons named Will and Mark and one was a year older and one was a year younger than I was. So, on their way home from the walk, they stopped back by and invited me to come down and see the finished house and introduced me to their boys and had me stay for dinner.

After that first evening, there weren't many days that I didn't go down there. It became a safe place for me. I could go over there and never feel unwanted. I was never turned away. This new family became my second family and my home away from home. Will and I quickly became friends. I will always consider him my best friend. We can go years without talking and come back together and it's like no time has passed. His parents and I continued to speak a couple times a year until the last few years.

On the 4th of July we'd have a great night in the cul-de-sac, and then the next morning we all had to go and clean all the fireworks up and sweep and clean the whole street. It was an all-day project that I never looked forward to, but it was all part of such a fun tradition. I remember how my dad and all the neighbors would light off fireworks and we used to ride our bikes down the street and some of the other kids would try and shoot bottle rockets into the spokes of our bike tires to make us crash.

In elementary school there was this girl named Audrey who lived at the bottom of the hill, and she and I would hang out after school. My mom or dad would drop me off at the bottom of the hill and let us play together. It was a blast with her, and we always had a connection. Her mom was a stay-at-home mom who was really fun to hang around with. Her stepdad worked for Pepsi as a driver, so there was always Pepsi at their house.

Audrey also became friends with Will and Mark when they moved into their finished home. With only two houses separating all of us, we became the best of friends and were inseparable... not knowing what our friendship would later endure. We would do everything together, so our mothers gave us the nickname: The Cul-de-Sac Rats, since we didn't do much besides hang around our little piece of the neighborhood.

All the Rats were in school when the shooting happened at Thurston High School. We didn't know who had been killed yet, so we showed up at Audrey's house, waiting to see if we'd all made it home alive. Once we knew that everyone in our group was safe, we turned on the news. It was showing the fence in front of the school being lined with flowers and notes from the community.

News coverage was all about the school, up and down the halls, showing videos of the injured and of students being walked out of the school by FBI agents. By that afternoon, our school fence was completely covered. It was the craziest thing I had ever seen.

At this fence there was so much emotion and I thought of fellow students that I saw during the shooting and was not sure if they had survived or not. It brought the four of us much closer.

Two months after the school shooting, on August 4, my father committed suicide in his cop car at 9:05 a.m. I was in Seattle at the time, visiting family. My mom called and told me my dad had been killed in the line of duty. After the longest car ride in history, I went to Audrey's house. The news media was covering my home, and when I was there, they kept asking me how he died. My mom wouldn't allow me to watch the TV. Obviously, everyone else knew that he had committed suicide, but my mother had yet to tell me. I didn't find out until later what had really happened. Another moment that changed me forever.

The Cul-de-Sac Rats spent many summers together playing flashlight tag all over the hill we lived on, celebrated birthdays, went to school, graduated and now are all in different places all over the world. I look back and think of how awesome our life was, despite living through our trauma.

We had some unforgettable nights under the stars. If we were ever together again, I could see it being just like no time had passed…we would all carry on just as it was back then. I hope and wish every one of them is well and staying safe, and I hope that their kids find friends like they were for me.

My Father

One of the first memories I have of my dad is when I was about four years old, sitting on the couch looking out the front window, watching it snow. From the kitchen, my mom yelled, "Your dad is coming home!" I sat by the fire and waited for his Sheriff's white Ford Bronco to arrive.

I remember seeing his Bronco and running outside as my mom told me, "Not without shoes!" and I went tumbling down the driveway to end up at my dad's feet. He picked me up, went inside, and we cuddled up on the couch, and watched TV.

In elementary school, my dad was the local Sherriff. One of his responsibilities was doing the D.A.R.E. (Drug Abuse Resistance Education) program. He would come to our school and educate us on the danger of drugs, along with the classic Smokey the Bear fire danger warning. My dad always had this big briefcase full of drug paraphernalia, and he would sit me up on stage while he talked. It was a pretty cool feeling. Afterwards, we'd have lunch together.

I went bow hunting with my dad one time and one time only. He had never caught a deer, but he was going deer hunting, and I decided to go with him to see what it was all about. We were hiking through the woods, and I remember him telling me to sit still and that there was a deer ahead. He pulled his bow into an arch and was getting ready to shoot the deer, and I made a noise on purpose and started to break the branch I was stepping on. I saved Bambi, but my dad was pretty upset with me. I was never allowed to go with him again. Fortunately, we had other things we did together.

After my parents' divorce, my dad would come and pick me up and take me to baseball games once in a while. He would pick me up in front of my mom's house, and we would go to a Hawaiian restaurant in downtown Eugene and then we'd go to the game. After the game we'd head to Farrell's Ice Cream Parlour. Those were really good times.

I remember that in elementary and middle school, my dad would show up with balloons and candy at the school awards ceremony as I always seemed to get an award for something. I was always excited to see him out in the audience holding the balloon in his sheriff's uniform, standing next to my mom.

I remember my dad having yellow roses sent to my mom at least once a month, or he would bring a bouquet home from work. Now that I'm older, I know that it was probably because he was having an affair, but back then, I just saw it as a loving gesture.

My dad and I would go down to Thurston Park by the high school, and we would shoot some hoops. He really wanted me to get into sports even though it was pretty obvious that it wasn't going to happen. But I thought it would make him happy, so I tried to shoot hoops while he ran the track. It was incredibly boring, but it was time with my dad.

For my birthdays in July, we'd go camping near Clear Lake. Year after year, we'd set up our tent in someone else's reserved spot because my dad would never stop to check the spots. And then after unloading and getting camp ready, my dad would realize that our spot was not actually available, and we would have to move as soon as the other people showed up.

One of my very favorite things to do was ride around with my dad in his squad car during one of his shifts. I would go with him before work, and he would go work out at the gym, and then he would go shower, and I would polish his boots. He would then get out of the shower and do some other things like shave, and I would just sit there and ask him questions about how many 911 calls we were going to get and other things about his job.

I remember my dad getting all ready and looking down at me, and he would give me the fake badge that he had for me while I was "working" with him. He would pin it to my jacket and that's how I knew we were ready to go. We would head down to the briefing room where we met all the other officers and got handed our work for the shift…and then off to the car we would go.

After that, I would ride a long ten-hour shift with my dad and he would do things like hand out warrants, or we would sit for hours tracking people's speed on the highway, pulling people over and issuing citations. I loved my dad and really looked up to him, not just because he was an officer of the law, but because he was a really good dad.

August 4, 1998

I always spent part of the summer in Seattle with my aunt and uncle. While they went to work, I would watch their daughter. I remember waking up around 8:30 a.m. because my aunt and I used to play Tomb Raider all night long on the PS2. My cousin would wake up soon after and we would have breakfast together. But the really great part was that they had a pool. Every day for the entire summer, I would go out to the pool and swim for hours upon hours. After so much time in the sun, I would be so dark that we didn't look like we were part of the same family. I always had a lot of fun. These were some of the best moments of my childhood. Just carefree, lazy summer days with my extended family.

On August 4th at around noon, my aunt and my uncle both returned home from work early, which was very unusual. I was in the pool with my cousin and when they came home, they just kind of shuffled to the back of the living room. I didn't think anything of it at the time, and I just kept on swimming. Swimming in that pool was a place where I could forget about what had happened at Thurston that year. When I had too much time to think, I would relive that moment. I was kind of stuck with the PTSD and the thoughts and the sounds of gunshots and students running and screaming and seeing the blood drip all over the walls and the ground. I was stuck in that moment for so long, I often didn't realize what reality really was.

Reality was about to hit me, hard. When my aunt and uncle both came out of the room, they came out back with their heads down. My uncle was a 6'4" ex-football player, and my aunt was about 5'10" and just a kick-ass woman; always in a good mood, always smiling. Seeing them looking so distraught, I knew something was very, very wrong. They both came outside, walked over to me and he said, "We need you inside."

I remember having a feeling in my gut of 'oh no, here we go I'm only 15 and another bad thing.' What else can happen to me? Why is this happening to me and when the fuck is it going to stop? I slowly got out of the pool and wrapped myself in a towel and walked inside with my cousin, and my aunt and uncle were sitting down in the front room. I sat down and just looked around as the room stayed awkwardly silent. It was silent for about two minutes before I heard my aunt sniffle and I saw tears in my uncle's eyes. I'd never seen my aunt or my uncle cry.

My stomach knotted and my mind started having these racing thoughts. I wasn't sure what it was that I didn't know, but something very bad was coming. My immediate family was all down in Oregon, and I was in Seattle with my aunt and uncle. I felt unsteady and unsure. Finally, my uncle broke the silence when he burst out in tears and said, "Your father has died."

The knot in my stomach dropped to the ground, my brain stopped thinking thoughts, and my heart stopped beating and fell out of my chest onto the ground by my stomach. There was nothing anyone could do. I looked at my aunt and I said, "This is true?" She said yes, and they both started crying. They both got up to give me a hug and I just remember running…running out into the backyard, past the pool, into the garden and just falling on the ground.

Tears streamed down my face with a feeling of emptiness I'd never felt before; a feeling of anxiety I'd never even imagined, and all I wanted to do was die and be with my dad. I wanted to jump up to the stars and grab him and hold him and have him tell me that he loves me. I sat there for a couple hours until my aunt and uncle came out. It was just so hard. I loved my father. I loved him very much. I still do.

They offered to drive me back to Oregon, and they told me that my father's funeral would be four days later, and they were making arrangements. They told me he died in the line of duty. During a very, very, very long drive of about five hours down to Eugene from Seattle, all I remember from that car ride was anxiety, tears, emptiness, and my aunt and uncle looking in the rear-view mirror the whole time, watching me cry with tears in their own eyes, which made me cry even more. I remember stopping and getting food and not wanting to eat but I did anyway, and I threw it up.

We couldn't get home fast enough and, of course, there

was road construction down I-5. And then we were home too soon. I remember pulling up to my grandma's side of the duplex where we lived and there were so many people out in front of my house. I just wanted to go to my grandma's house and be alone and wait for my mom and my brother and my family.

I remember sitting there waiting, and I remember my mother walking in, and I just lost it when I saw the pain in her eyes. My brother walked in and even though he and I didn't always get along, at that moment it didn't matter as we recognized that we had both just lost our father. My brother was much closer to him than I was, but that doesn't change the fact that both of us had just had our world shattered.

I remember going down to my neighbor Audrey's house, wanting to just say Hi, and everybody there would not really tell me what was going on, but I knew something was. I wasn't allowed to watch TV. I was told not to talk to certain people, and I was definitely not allowed to go outside. I wasn't allowed to read the newspaper, nothing. It was strange and eerie. There was an air of mystery, but all I could do was grieve.

Six hours later, at 3 in the morning, I was still crying my eyes out, so when my mom came in from the other room and asked me if I was okay, I replied with, "Absolutely not." I remember her holding my hand as I leaned forward and she sat down next to me and said, "I need to tell you about how your father died."

My heart got even heavier, and the anxiety came, and my

head started spinning and I said out loud, "Oh my God," and she said, "Your father committed suicide. He put a gun to his head, and he blew his head off."

And once again, I ran out of the room and started crying even more. Obviously, my enormous abandonment issues started there. I felt utterly and completely alone. An hour later, I was still sitting there on the floor, lost in my head, crying out for my father, knowing that I'd never hear his voice, knowing that I'd never feel his touch and knowing that I'd never, ever be able to see his face again. My mother came upstairs later that day and handed me a note. I opened the note and read:

My beautiful boys, this is not your fault. I am so proud of you. I will be watching down on you from Heaven with Grandma D, and I want you boys to love each other and take care of your mother and be the men that I know you can be. I never meant to hurt you, but I'll always be looking down on you from Heaven.
Love, your father.

We also found out that he had put his badge in the mail, along with a couple thousand dollars to help pay for his funeral, so this was obviously planned out in advance. He shot himself at 9:05 a.m. on August 4th. I thought about how little I had seen him that year due to the fact that he left my mom and asked for a divorce. There were things going on between my parents that I was too young to understand. The morning of the school shooting in May was the last time I ever saw him.

As it turns out, at 9:04 a.m. on August 4, my father tried calling me in Seattle to tell me that he loved me. I didn't realize that would be the last time he ever tried to call me, and that it would be the last time his number would pop up in my caller ID, but I was outside and didn't take the call. He shot himself thirty seconds after that phone call. Death is strange. It eats you alive with guilt. What if I had picked up the phone and said I love you? What if I had picked it up and said you're a great dad? What if I could have stopped him from killing himself? I don't know if it actually had that strong an influence, but among my last words to my father, a year earlier, were "Fuck you." I don't even remember why I was so angry or why I lashed out this way.

I will forever regret saying those words to my father. I will always wish I hadn't, but I accept my choices. I've chosen to be more forgiving of myself and my father and today, right now, at this very moment I would not change anything in my life.

My father loved me, and I loved my father. He's a part of me and I'm a part of him and I will do my best to represent him, and I'll do my best to be someone he'd be proud of. I feel as if I can still talk to him and have a full conversation and hear his response. I'm thankful that I had my father for so many years. But if I could talk to him now, I would ask him: Why did you do it just two months after the shooting, when one of my friends walked in and opened fire on my school? Don't you think that was enough?

My Mother

My mother and I had a close but somewhat volatile relationship. There are so many things I adore and respect about my mother. She worked her way up from nothing in her job at the school district to one that she hadn't even dreamed of. She was a professional success. She married my father and did her best to keep that relationship healthy and secure. She made sure that we boys were cared for, that we stayed on top of our homework, and that we did chores around the house. She was a strong lady for going through the divorce with my father and despite being broke and alone she still put food on the table and made sure everything that her sons needed was provided.

The relationship I had with my mother was intense. I used to regularly ask my dad for money to buy my mom a flower that I would put on the front seat of her car just so she would be surprised and would know that I loved her and how grateful I was for her. I remember her baking gingerbread houses for Christmas that went the full length of the piano. She was always in the kitchen either baking or cooking, and instead of going hunting with my dad, I would stay at home with my mom. There were times we were inseparable, and when I was younger, she always had my back. But after my father left and filed for divorce, I changed, my mother changed. My whole family changed.

The following years were more stressful than I could have imagined. My dad left and filed for divorce. Mom was so broke and poor we could barely survive, but we did. Our first Christmas alone without our dad was tough, then came a new year beginning on the wrong foot, then the tragedy hit: a school shooting which directly involved me and my family and friends, followed by my father's suicide two months later. I understand now how much my mother had to deal with. And she was already bitter about him leaving us down and out after filing for divorce.

Knowing my father was out there starting a new relationship was really hard on my mom. She was left to work a full-time job and raise two young men who missed their dad, working hard to keep our home afloat, not showing any sign of despair or anger and always moving forward until she was back up on her feet and could stand proud. I didn't realize how hard he'd made her life until later.

I was taken aback by my dad asking my mom for divorce. I didn't know what to think about it, and I wasn't sure what I was supposed to do about it. The last thing any child wants is to see their parents get a divorce. I remember sitting at my uncle's house in Seattle with my mom when she got that call from my father. I remember my mom dropping the phone to the floor and curling over in screams and tears. She continued to cry, and my aunt and uncle tried calming her down, but nothing could take away the pain that she felt at that time. I was told later that by the time we would be back from vacation, my dad would be completely moved out and he would be living and starting a life with someone else. It was a horrible drive home. I still hate the drive from Seattle to Eugene. Those next couple days, mom was crying, playing sad songs, and the whole way home was one last memory of when we were a family.

When we got back home, we sat there for a minute in the driveway, and my mom started to cry again. I wasn't sure how I would react going in and not seeing my dad's stuff there. I recall my grandmother coming from the other side of the duplex and I saw our dog sitting at the fence waiting impatiently for some pets and love as I was sure the energy had changed in the house with my dad leaving.

My dad and our dog were very close, and I suspected that the dog was having a super hard time. I was right, the dog was definitely not having it. She would not eat or drink for several days after my dad left. A few short weeks later, our dog passed away and it was one of the saddest days because it was one of the few things that held the memory of my father at the house; her barking every time that he pulled into the driveway.

We finally got the courage to go inside and start the next chapter of our lives as a family of three. I didn't realize it, but now looking back I blamed my mother for it all. I blamed her for dad leaving, for us not having money, barely paying our bills—

and did I ever let her have it. I also made sure she knew the hurt and anger along with the frustration I had and was holding against her. I was in pain and lashed out at the person who was there.

Over the next year we did not see my dad very much and my mom wanted to minimize contact. I still to this day regret not taking a stance and saying how much I wanted to see my dad. For a while, every phone call was blocked, and every message was screened, as if my dad was completely non-existent. I took it out on my mom on a daily basis; yelling, screaming and disrespecting her every single day.

Then the divorce court date came, and my father was awarded time with us boys. I remember seeing my dad for the first time after being ripped away from him. We went to a baseball game and it was so good to see him. I remember him driving his truck to the house and pulling around the cul-de-sac and then waiting for me to run out. He gave me a huge hug, and I felt such excitement. I thought a new chapter had begun. I was happy and thought that maybe life would be getting back to normal.

My dad offered to start picking me up and taking me to school in the morning since he worked out at the gym right down the street from where I went to school. He would pick me up at 7:50 a.m. with breakfast in hand and he would drop me off at 7:56. On the morning of the shooting, we were in that same routine, and little did he and or anyone know that something was about to upend our lives again.

He dropped me off at 7:45 this time and I went to the music room. I was sitting there not really do anything when I heard the gun fire start. I called my mom in tears and terror saying "Mom, someone has a gun in the school, and they're shooting everyone! Please, send Dad to save me, please!" An hour later, my father came and found me. I grabbed onto him, and I never wanted to let go. But because of the divorce and the visitation agreement, all he could do was drive me to my mom. That was the last time I ever saw him.

From that day forward, once again my mother's and my relationship changed forever. I blamed her for everything. I was not sleeping at night, I wanted to feel safe and have my dad come back home and he couldn't, and I blamed her for all of it. I didn't realize how much anger I had against my mother until later on in life.

I called her fat. I told her she was ugly. After dad committed suicide, I told her she made my father kill himself. I told her if she had lost weight that my dad might still be alive. I would throw it in her face every single day. That she murdered my father. That she destroyed my life and our family.

I have sincerely apologized for all of it, and I have tried to make things right, but unfortunately the damage is done. I spent years of my time blaming her. I still to this day can feel how much hatred I once carried for her. When the judge granted my dad visitation rights, I thought everything was going to be all right. But it never was.

Two months after the school shooting, my father committed suicide on the job in his police car. After all of this, my mother and I have had a strained relationship. There are times I go months and months without contacting her. Sometimes years. I hate that every time we are together, we fight. I say things and she says things that should never be said to someone you love. And I realize that our relationship will never be the way it was. But I do respect the fact that she gave birth to me. That she tried so hard. That she loved me the best she could. I am grateful for everything she did and finally, I can let go of the past with a smile and a grateful heart. Recently, we have started to reconnect. Though I can't predict what the future holds, and it will take much effort from both of us, I do believe that we can rebuild a relationship. At least I hope so.

Coffee Shop Girl

It was January, the middle of winter. I was 22 years old. I'd been laid off from a local grocery store, and I was looking for work. I came across a small coffee shop which was looking for help, and out of the 26 people who applied, I got the job. Brewing coffee and serving customers seemed to be an atmosphere I might thrive in and do well in, so I was excited about the job. The owners were very happy with my work ethic.

What I didn't know was that one of the owners had worked at the county sheriff's office, which is where my father used to work before his suicide. I had not been face-to-face with anyone associated with this office since my dad's death. The county workers had always promised to come and visit us kids and take care of us and watch over us, but not one single person from the department ever did.

While I was working at the coffee shop, the owners' family members would come in and they were always kind and seemed to really like me. I worked my ass off there, and because they knew who I was and who my dad was, they were very aware of my PTSD and everything that I had been through. They accommodated me the best they could. My coworkers were great, and I worked hard every day. I made enough money to cover my rent and my bills. Everything was going well, and it honestly didn't even cross my mind to be prepared for more trauma and more drama.

In the spring of that year, I got the news that my friend Daniel had been killed in a logging accident. The owners of the coffee shop were so kind to me, covering my shifts and looking out for me while I grieved this loss. What they didn't realize, is that I was back to using drugs to numb the pain, so I couldn't come in to work even if I had wanted to.

Daniel was a good man and a good friend with no enemies and smiles for everybody. He was so funny, so high energy and so positive. He taught me how to fish, he took me camping, he taught me how to hunt, how to drive a stick shift, and many other things. Basically, he taught me how to have fun and how to let go of anger. As devastating as it was to see our friend pass away, he brought the old group back together. His death brought friends who were fighting back together and got them to recognize the power of love.

Daniel's funeral was heart-wrenching. Over 300 people showed up and it was one of the hardest days of my life. After the funeral, we all drove up and went to the gravesite to watch him be buried. The depression I felt was limitless, as if I had fallen into a dark pit. Again, a man who I looked up to, who I was close to, who I loved was gone from my life.

Later, my co-worker Christine visited the gravesite with me, and that's where and when we got together. I was in a vulnerable state and needed someone to lean on. She had a smile that lit up my world, and anytime she came over, she took care of me. But after a while, I was so broken that I started to act out and get angry with her. I knew that we should be growing stronger and spending more time together, as I really didn't know what I would do without her. My moods were in conflict, needing Christine to be close, but at the same time behaving in a way that pushed her away.

Later that month, the coffee shop decided to let me go. They fired me when I couldn't make my shifts because I was so depressed. Christine continued to work there, and she took over the rent payments on my apartment, and she even lent me some money to get by. But there was one night in July where I just couldn't take life anymore.

I knew that I was supposed to get myself together and go to Christine's that night for dinner with her family. Instead, I sat in my room screaming and crying, and I decided to kill myself by taking sleeping pills and anti-anxiety pills. I ended up overdosing. If it seems odd that I had access to so many prescriptions, it was simply the doctors' best idea about treating me, without really understanding how to treat someone who had witnessed a mass shooting followed by their father's suicide.

I called Christine in anguish, telling her that I was done with life. When she heard this, she came over to my house and she found the front door locked and she couldn't get into my house. Since I was pretty much passed out upstairs, she actually climbed up on the roof of my place, came through my bedroom window, dragged me down the stairs, threw me in the back of her Jeep and took me to the hospital. At that point, I apparently started becoming a raving lunatic, but I have no memory of it. It took several doctors to pin me down and several pairs of straps to tie me down, and they put me into an induced coma.

While I was in that state, I do remember some things. My uncle reading from the Bible, John: 4, Christine's voice and the smell of her perfume, and I remember my mother coming and visiting me. I remember friends and family coming in, but the sound I recall most vividly is the rattle of a dog's chain when Christine either brought it in or wore it around her neck.

It seemed like I was out for just a minute and then one morning I opened my eyes and I saw a machine breathing for me, tubes down my throat, my hands tied to the bed, but my mood was still dark, and I managed to lift my fingers and flip off the nurses as they would look in on me. I did the same when they came into the room and would tell me to calm down and to breathe into the machine and that they would get me off that as soon as possible. I felt trapped, having been in a coma for 14 days. They didn't know if I was going to fully come out of it since I took so many pills.

Being in the hospital for a couple of weeks and then recovering, visiting with friends and family, having people come in and visit me was hardly the highlight of my life, but it did show me that having a strong and caring woman by my side was way better than being alone. Christine was by my side the entire time, and she took care of my dog, and she cleaned my house.

Christine got everything done. She was the best. She made the transition home easy. When she told me how she would always go home from work, then shower and get cleaned up, and put her makeup on and do her hair just to visit me when I was in that coma, it made me love her even more.

I finally got released and went home, I tried to get back on my feet, but I struggled, and Christine was always there. She told me right then that I had the chance to leave Oregon and move to California with her, and I was really excited. I definitely needed a change and a fresh start. My grandfather lived near Los Angeles, so I wouldn't be without family.

California Life

I was living in Colton, California with my uncle, my grandpa, and his wife. The first week, it was absolutely perfect, with big dinners and family time, meeting members of the family that I had never met before and about whom I had only heard stories. I was sitting at the dinner table with my grandpa, and I asked if I could go grab some dinner and he pulled me aside and asked me if I wanted to start working for him at the construction company that they'd had there in Colton for over 25 years.

Obviously, I said, yes. I did not want to let my family down again. I wanted to change. I wanted to build a future for myself and for my family. I believed I could turn things around…that I could be the "Comeback Kid."

Monday morning, I had to get up and go to work and be prepared to bust my ass. That meant getting up at 7 a.m. and working at 8:30. I remember getting in the work truck with my uncle and heading to the first construction site. I was nervous and excited all at once and I remember pulling up to this house in Redlands, CA. I was excited to see one of my grandfather's businesses come to life, and also, I was excited to start helping with the final process of the job and cleaning up the construction site. I was working all day long helping my uncle, and we worked a 9.5-hour day.

By the end of the day, I was exhausted. All I wanted to do was go home, lie down, and sleep. When the day ended, we went back to the house, turned in the work truck, signed our timecards, and went upstairs from the office to start the evening...except I was so tired I fell asleep at the dinner table. I had never worked so hard in my life. I continued dozing off before and during dinner, and then I finally went to bed right after dinner. I remember waking up the next morning and being so sore and so tired. It was just so hard physically to get up and start moving again.

I continued this schedule for several weeks before transferring and moving towards L.A. to be with my fiancée Christine, who was at school at USC. Once it became clear that my grandparents and I did not share the same opinions on religion and a few other topics, I finally got the guts to move out of Colton and on to new adventures. I think that what I learned from the experience is that I am able to do physically challenging manual labor, but it is definitely not my first choice. I was still finding myself, and I needed to be exposed to other career options. Later, I found that being a personal assistant or a personal caregiver really suited me a lot better. I feel best when I am helping others.

California Tremors

Looking back on my first move to L.A., I can see that I was too young and too unprepared to really make it work. I was all about having fun rather than seeking out stability. After we arrived, my fiancée Christine got settled in at USC and I went and visited her. It was fun to live the college experience, since I did not attend college except for two years at a community college in Oregon.

Walking around, I was starstruck, watching the football team practice and being in downtown Los Angeles for the first time — seeing all the glitz and glamour everywhere. We spent several days going to the beach, walking around Hollywood, getting my first taste of Beverly Hills luxury fashion and the upscale life I had always seen in movies but never in real life. I couldn't stay with Christine in her dorm room because she only had a twin bed, and her roommate was not cool with it. I ended up sleeping in the back of Christine's Jeep in the parking garage of her dorm.

Christine and I started to argue and fight more, finances were tight, and she was about to start school. The first couple of days of her first term, I was left behind in the back of her

Jeep, waiting for her to come and unlock the doors to the dorm so I could go up and take a shower or get some food with her. We always seemed to end up fighting. I didn't understand the hard work she needed to put in and didn't allow her the space to get it done. Since she had so much homework, she started to fall behind very quickly. She wanted to experience college life, and the parties, and I just wanted to find a job, find a home and settle down. Eventually, it wore us out, and we went our separate ways after a few intense moments and the exchange of some ugly words. But without her support, things for me were about to go from bad to worse.

I ended up checking myself into the hospital in L.A. because I was emotionally overwhelmed. Since I had tried taking my own life a couple of times before, I knew the warning signs of what was about to happen if I didn't get help. I went to the hospital and told them that I was suicidal and automatically they put me on a week-long hold in a mental institution in Cerritos, which was terrifying.

Waking up every morning in a sterile room, wearing paper clothes with a 7:00 a.m. med call, then sitting around all day with only smoking breaks outside, staring at walls thirty feet high and a security guard who watched my every move isn't how you really want to spend your day.

People were walking around like zombies, fights were breaking out, we could not even use real silverware. I could only use a toothbrush made out of paper and I wasn't allowed to shave myself. Evidently either of these tools could be used as a weapon. After a week of that, I was back to sleeping in the back of Christine's car, and during the day I did what I had to do to survive.

Because of my PTSD, I was eligible for government grants, and I registered myself for a community college in Riverside. My desire to improve myself was strong, even if my study skills were not. College proved to be the same challenge as high school. Being a non-normal learner didn't fit well in our educational systems of the time. The housing department at the college sent me to live in an apartment in Marina del Rey with four college athletes I didn't know.

By Thanksgiving, I could see that this living situation was not going to work out, and that sent me over the edge once more. I overdosed on Tylenol and got myself sent to an even stricter mental ward back in Cerritos, where I stayed for two weeks on suicide watch. The cycle was repeating itself, but somehow, I survived, and moved on to somewhere else.

Understanding Trauma

It was years before I actually noticed much change in myself. Honestly. At first, I was so stuck in my head that I didn't realize what I actually had was Post Traumatic Stress Disorder. I was sleeping some, but not enough. My social skills did not change much; I always had the same small group of friends and that was it. I was able to go out in public with no problems. I did not have much change in my life immediately after the shooting. When August hit and my father killed himself is when I started to have a harder time, but still things were going alright as far as I knew. I didn't realize that it was all just the beginning stages of a lifelong battle with night terrors, social anxiety, and a fear-based life.

I started noticing that I'd changed from sleeping kind of okay to not sleeping at all. The nightmares started to get worse and worse, and the images got more vivid as time went on. I have no way to measure the change between May 21st and August 4th of 1998, and life after my father's suicide. But the change was extreme. The lack of security of losing a parent is one of the hardest things that you can ever experience. I don't know if it's better if you see it coming, but I don't really think it's something any of us can prepare for. It's like a safety net is taken away where we are thrown out into the world in the midst of the unknown arena of making our own decisions, while not having a person to rely on at the other end of a phone call. On that horrible day in May, my father came when I was able to call him to get me out of school after the shooting. I'll remember forever seeing his face and knowing I was going to be okay. This is the security I felt when he walked in, the anxiety that melted away when I saw him, and he embraced me.

On August 4, when my father killed himself, that meant that he was gone. I had no one to really turn to. My mother wasn't very present. At the time, she was going through her own things, and my brother and I were not very close. Friends stopped by, but I was still traumatized by the shootings. As time went on and we had the first Christmas, the first Thanksgiving, the first Easter without my father, things got to be very real in knowing that I would never have that security blanket back. Nightmares got more vivid, and I was not understanding why I didn't want to go out in public. I was so depressed and so anxiety ridden that I didn't know what to do with myself.

At 15, I was already traumatized by two life-shaking events, and I had no idea where to go, what to do, who to turn to. So, I shut down. I didn't turn to my friends; I isolated myself in my room or in my house and sometimes I didn't even go to school. When I did, I hid behind my saxophone so I wouldn't have to interact with anyone. I had a hard time going to school. I had a hard time being around people, a hard time communicating, and a hard time socializing.

It felt like I was just dead inside on some levels. I felt as though everyone had their own agendas. Sometimes people don't get it when it looks like I'm present, but I'm not. Everyone was moving on and leaving me behind. Everyone had their own lives and here I was, stuck in my own body, in my own head, trapped inside with no one to turn to who understood me.

As I got older, I realized how hard it is for me to hold down a job. Every time I'd get ready for work, I would get this weight in my chest, and I would start breathing heavily. When I got off work, I would be so happy, but knowing I had to go back the next day killed me on the inside. The anxiety was crippling.

Even when I had to go to public events like baseball games or to a bar, the anxiety just killed me. It took me hours to get ready; it took me hours to prepare myself to go out in public, and I used every excuse in the book not to go.

It wasn't that I didn't want to go. It's that I didn't know how to be safe out in public. I didn't know what to do with myself, feeling so vulnerable in any place that was not in my total control. I started to realize little things about myself; things that I didn't know were inflicted on me by those two events, such as a need to be in control of my environment, constantly changing my environment, rearranging my room and constantly cleaning, making sure everything was perfect. As though those things would make me safe.

With time, I realized that the reason I did all that was because I was not in control of the shootings or when my dad committed suicide. I had no idea that being in control of my environment was a part of PTSD and I had no idea that being in my head as much as I was, and still am to this day, is a full-time job in itself. People always ask me, "What's wrong? Why are you staring off into space?" It's because I'm in my head — images, emanations, visions of the future, visions of the past, they all hit my brain all at once. Sometimes it's so overwhelming that I don't even know what to do with myself. This often happens in the middle of the night. Sometimes I have to call a friend, just to feel safer, just to feel sane, or just to feel heard. Sometimes I don't know what to do and I freak out. I'm trying to control those things but even more than twenty years later, it's hard.

I now have my service dogs, Nido and Timo, and they do such a great job — when I'm having a hard time, they come up to me. When I am afraid, they sense it. When I am in panic or depression mode, they lift me up. I love my dogs. Yes, they are expensive, particularly when you're broke because you can't hold down a job. Owning any pet is expensive. But they earn their keep many times over by staying by my side every time I am stuck in my head, dealing with the effects of the trauma I went through.

My nightmares are subsiding. Slowly but surely, I am becoming a man who can be productive and find my own answers to problems. It is the power of my honest truth that has kept me alive. It took one person to believe in me and with that I am very strong and content within myself, the world I make, and my home, and who I am when I look in the mirror.

My nightmares are still there. My trauma is still there. But I defy my trauma by using the lessons life has taught me and by being vulnerable and calling on my dogs and a few friends and all of them being there for me. I stand tall today. I will not be defined by my trauma. Yes, I struggle, but every day I am a little more successful. It helps so much when even one person believes in you, but you must believe in yourself as well.

Justin

The story of Justin begins when I was 21. My older brother started dating a girl named Laura. Laura was from the same city, but she went to another high school. She and my brother dated for about two years off and on. She and I became close as friends. When my brother would go to work, we would sit around and smoke weed every morning, getting high as a kite, and then I would go to work at Albertson's grocery store. We became pretty close as friends, and it felt like we were family members until they broke up. Five years went by before I saw her again.

One day, thanks to social media, I found Laura on Facebook, and I reached out. I went over to her house and saw her parents and met with her and then we lost contact again for a couple years. So once again, when I moved back home from California, I hit her up and she told me that she had a kid. A young boy named Justin. Little did I know that moment in time would change my life. I met Laura at a local park across the street from a shopping center. As I walked into the park, I saw her, and we embraced and just started talking.

I heard this little 4-year-old boy screaming and hollering

and I told her, "That must be your child. Sounds just like you." She laughed and said, "Yes."

Justin was a bit out of sorts, visibly uncomfortable. Definitely suffering from some sensory overload. As the day went on, we went out to lunch, and I noticed that Justin clearly had some issues. A lack of eye contact and repetitiveness and also an infatuation with certain objects.

I'm not a doctor, but I'm pretty sure he had autism or at least was on the autism spectrum. I didn't want to say anything, since it seemed rude to diagnose someone else's child, but as the day went on, Laura confirmed my suspicion. That is when my connection with him began. I began spending time with this child, and it came naturally to me to try to help him to handle different stimuli.

Justin's father was no longer present in his life. It seemed like his father was using him pretty much for the social security check. He and Laura did not get along, and Justin's dad hated me. He hated me because I was getting his son to advance and to learn how to cope with certain sensory overload symptoms by giving him tools to put in his toolbox to use.

I finally moved into Laura's parents' house to help them take care of Justin, as well as his two cousins Emily and Sarah, who were also placed under my charge. Laura went to work on a daily basis and so did I, and we would switch off on watching Justin because he was a handful for the grandparents and everyone else to watch. It wasn't a formal arrangement, but I did it because I felt like I belonged in this role. I could see that this child was getting shuffled around between caregivers and he and his family needed help.

Laura was not even living on the same side of town as her parents. She and her boyfriend had their own apartment. Kids need consistency and Justin got some of that consistency in the form of me being there all the time. Helping him learn to cope with the world around him. It was something I discovered I loved doing. Helping this kid learn to tackle a world that he didn't understand…and that didn't understand him.

Eventually, I got a boyfriend. He was pretty cool at first and after about six months we moved in together. I was a little hesitant letting Justin get taken to school by my guy, but after school, it was back to Justin and me. And it was me who Justin would come to when he was in trouble. There were times when he would hit himself in the head and he would even choke himself, leaning up against the kitchen counter. I knew I was only giving him foster care, but I took to this job of parenting very quickly and easily.

One day, I was at the mall and I got a phone call. It was the school saying that they needed to see me immediately. I went driving to the school as fast as I could. I walked in and there were the teachers in one room and Justin isolated in the other, crying, screaming, hollering at Laura.

His mother had also been notified but she'd been pulled aside and was not allowed to see her son. The yelling, the screaming of a mother that was not able to see her child is one of the worst sounds I've ever heard. But the screaming of a child wanting to see his mother is even worse. As I was pulled aside, I was told that when Justin came to school, he was wearing a turtleneck and he wouldn't take it off, even though the weather was warm.

As a teacher went by, she noticed red marks on his neck, scratches, and so she continued to talk to him and he finally said, "Fine...You want to see it? My stepdad choked me because I wrote on the walls with a crayon." The teacher immediately took action and had Justin pulled aside. They called the school principal, and Child Protective Services (CPS) was called. At that point in time, the mother was not allowed to see her child until the formal statement was made.

After that, Laura denied these accusations and told them Justin was lying, not the stepdad. I was asked to take custody of Justin and take him home and keep him safe. Of course, I said yes. And as I said yes, Laura was livid because I had to keep her from her son and not allow her at the house. Not allow her to even talk to him. Nothing.

As time went by, Justin went to counseling every week, and CPS did a check of my house. They told me to lock up the knives. And they told me I had to put my medications up out of reach. CPS has a job to do, and they had to protect Justin. When Justin had to go to court and testify, his mother still denied the accusations and with her denying the accusations and standing by her boyfriend instead of her own son, it made her look very bad.

It got to the point where CPS wouldn't even allow her to see or talk to Justin. As we continued our weekly appointments, the counselor saw great improvements in Justin's behavior—both in the way he was reacting and the progress he was making in school. I was that boy's 'father' for a very long time.

Eventually Justin was allowed to talk to Laura over the phone, which led to supervised visits at McDonald's or in public places. I got the worst vibes from Laura's boyfriend. She would sometimes look at me, snarl at me and say that she wanted time alone with Justin so he would hear their very different side of the story. She would kind of coach him, and I just couldn't allow it. It was a very difficult situation to be in. But I also had a job to do and that was to protect Justin and, damn it, I did, and I would do it over and over again.

I would sit at night and watch him sleep. Sometimes I would cry. I don't know how anyone could lay a hand on someone, let alone a child, a child that was seemingly coached to act as if he were on the spectrum for a social security check. A child who was possibly taught these behaviors just to be punished for them. A child that just wanted to be loved and wanted to spread the love all over the world. Justin would fall asleep at night holding my pinky finger, and I'd have to lay with him until he fell asleep. He always used to have to watch TV, but as time went on, we got him to go to sleep without it.

When I first met Justin, he only ate three things: Little Caesars pepperoni pizza, popcorn, and carrots. That changed too. As time went by, his grandparents and I got him to eat many other fruits and vegetables. The counselors at the CPS were astonished by his improvements. In just months, he was doing better in school. He was making friends. He was learning how to communicate. He was telling teachers how he was having sensory overload and he needed to have a minute. I had an Individual Education Program put in place so that he could succeed and not fail.

After a while Laura got rid of the boyfriend because she realized that it was the only way she was going to get her son back or at least get to see him again. I confess it was very hard to allow them to have outings together without me there because I felt like I couldn't protect him. I felt useless and helpless.

It was the worst feeling in the world. They had more and more visitations together without me, and I don't know how to explain it, but it was like watching my own child being ripped out of my arms just the way it was earlier from his mother except not so abruptly. I also continued to follow CPS guidelines and rules and started to let go a little bit of Justin. But I never stopped the consistency. I communicated everything to his mother, and I also went there and talked to her about maybe getting him into the water because she said he hated it.

I took him swimming one time and he liked it so much that we ended up going almost every day that summer. I knew from my summers in Seattle at my aunt and uncle's pool that the sensory experience of being in the water is soothing for those of us who have social coping issues. I got him into swimming lessons with his own personal swim coach, who later became my friend and roommate.

After a while, he saw potential in Justin that no one else ever had. He had Justin doing the butterfly stroke. And Justin was beating everyone on his team within three weeks. He was jumping off the high dive within a month, going down the slide by himself within weeks, and didn't need a life jacket after a month. He was so natural in the pools, from the deep water to the lap pool to the regular pools. He was finally doing everything like a normal kid and excelling at everything he tried.

Justin asked his mom to come to one of his swim classes and she did, and she hated it. She told me it was not allowed. She told me she was going to take him out of the group. She told me that she didn't want him to have that coach and she literally tried ripping swimming out of his life even though it was his main outlet for stress. He was sleeping at night. He would do his homework. He would eat well. He was everything that I thought he couldn't be when I first met him.

The day finally came when I had to return Justin to his mom. I was told that I would be able to see him. I was told I could call anytime and that I could stop by whenever I wanted; and as much as I wanted to believe it, I knew it wasn't true. I took Justin to his mom at their new apartment, and discovered his dad was back in the picture, which seemed strange.

I remember walking him in, and the whole time on the way there, he said, "I don't want to go there," and when he suddenly called me Dad, I lost it. I lost it to all ends of the earth. Tears came rolling out of my eyes and I don't know how to explain the feeling I had. I felt like I was dying inside but living in a body that I didn't want to inhabit; in a head space that made me want to commit suicide. I couldn't take it. I knew that I was going to walk him in, take a look around and walk out without him for the first time in years. That boy went everywhere with me, and I mean everywhere; from the doctor's to swimming to the Saturday Market. Protecting Justin was what I lived for.

Leaving that apartment and having that door shut and hearing him scream for me crushed me. I couldn't even drive due to that feeling. I will never forget it. I never want to relive it. I don't wish it on anybody. It's terrible. I felt like I gave up on him. I thought maybe I didn't fight hard enough. I felt like I had failed. I finally got the courage to drive home, and I ended up drinking myself half to death because at home there was nothing to do. No clothes. No laundry. No schoolwork to supervise. No school in the morning. No lunches to pack.

It was one of the hardest chapters of my life, but perhaps the most meaningful. I found out through this experience what I was really capable of, what I was meant to do. Since then, I have actively sought out caregiver jobs. I know that this is absolutely my biggest strength.

Emily

Emily was born in August, and I met her at six hours old. Her parents took her home and then a couple of days later, I started watching her on a daily basis because they needed help. From the moment she could barely grab my finger, she had my heart. The first time I held her I knew that she was going to be much more than just a friend's child. The father in me came out—protective, loving, caring.

I promised her and myself that nothing would ever happen to her on my watch. I didn't realize how much work it was to watch a baby until I had her in my care. She had an older sister named Sarah who used to come visit us, too. I used to rock Emily in my chair to sleep every day and she would cover my finger with her tiny fingers and hang on. I would fall asleep with her head on my chest. I've never felt such inner peace. It was one of those moments where I knew I was growing up. I mean, I was technically an adult, but when Emily came into my care it was all uphill from there. I was watching her, her sister, and a foster child named Justin all at the same time. As I was raising the kids, I was growing up myself.

After about a year and a half, she finally said my name. She smiled so big and then giggled. She slowly climbed into my arms and fell asleep. I was noticing that she was picking up my habits quite a bit; from my walk and my stance to the way I made my facial expressions, and I never knew that something like that could make you feel so happy. It really hit home that I needed to be a role model for her. When I would hold her, nothing else mattered. Every time she was outside, I was outside. When she slept, I would watch her or sleep right next to her, making sure she was okay when she woke up.

As she started getting a little bit older, the biggest thing in media was Lady Gaga—she liked watching her on TV with Justin basically every day—and that's how they would wake me up if I was still sleeping: singing her songs. Her little facial expressions, the way she would ask me for things, the way she looked at me, the way she got mad at me…it was all starting to just grow on me like she was my own.

As time went on, her parents were able to become freer, and they started spending more time with Emily and her sister Sarah—and then eventually they were able to take over all of their care. As always, I needed to escape to a different state or to a different city.

I will always remember that girl, though. She will never know how much she meant to me and what she did for me. Words can hardly describe how much joy this baby girl brought me and how much growing up I did…and how much I started to love life again after all the events of the past. It also shows the parental instinct that we all carry at one point in time. It didn't matter how bad my day was, when I came home and that little girl was there, and she would just run up to me and grab onto my neck and scream with glee and never let go, it would never be a bad night.

I took care of that little girl for 5 straight years, and those were the most memorable New Year's Eves of my life. Just to see her wake up at midnight to watch us bang pots and pans. I'll never forget it. I would do the same thing when I was a kid. Counting down to Thanksgiving, Christmas, New Year's will always bring fond memories of this precious time.

I will never forget you, Emily.

Mental Ward

I was 22, and I was still working at the little café. I remember having a complete mental breakdown and wanting to commit suicide, but even though I had attempted suicide several times before, I hadn't really wanted to die. So, I turned myself in to a local hospital and told them that I wanted to hurt myself, and I automatically got put on 72-hour hold. I remember that my fiancée at the time was wondering what was going on, and I didn't quite know what to tell her. I just told her that I didn't want to live anymore, and I was going through a very hard time.

I had just lost my best friend Daniel to a logging accident, and I was emotionally unstable with not much support from my family or many friends. She had heard it all before. She'd seen me struggling with how to even talk about what I felt. But on this day, I turned myself in to the hospital, and I remember them giving me a Xanax and some sort of shot in the arm. I don't remember very much after that for the night.

I woke up the next morning, and I was in a hospital bed in this small room, hands tied to the side of the bed and in a hospital gown. I remember the doctor coming in and asking me what was wrong, asking me if everything was okay, which obviously it wasn't. I remember getting out of bed after they released the tie downs, and I remember going into a little office and talking with two psychologists. I was served food but not allowed to watch TV. I wasn't ready to go to the group meetings. I wasn't ready to talk to any of the other patients in the unit. Then someone came down and mentioned the Johnson Unit, and I felt a cringe-worthy feeling coming over me because I knew that the Johnson Unit in our local hospital was for crazy people. I knew I wasn't crazy. I knew I was just very depressed.

After the meal, I ended up going out to the main lobby and there were people in there literally talking to the walls. One person tried to hurt the nurse and they had to straddle him and hold him down and give him an injection and then tie him to his bed. It was pretty scary. I don't really remember talking to anyone. I just wanted to disappear.

My fiancée came to see me, and I remember her sitting with me in the little room for about 25 minutes before she had to leave because visiting hours were over. I wanted to go home with her so badly that I cried and cried. But the state wouldn't let me go because I was there after I had told them that I wanted to hurt myself and if you tell someone you're going to hurt yourself or someone else, they automatically put you on a 72-hour hold. So, no matter how well I was doing, or at least how well I thought I was doing, I was stuck in this crazy ward for the next three days.

The next day, I went to a meeting and found that some other people were in a similar situation, so I decided to open up to them and they did the same. I told them about my PTSD and about the sudden loss of my friend and all the other struggles in my life at that time. We were all there for the same reason. It was nice to not feel so alone after that meeting. I went to my psychologist who said I could go home on the second day. I didn't really know where I would go, but I wasn't really too worried about that. I was more concerned about the fact that my family, my mom and brother, didn't want to help me; they just wanted to leave me sitting on the streets or sitting inside my apartment at the risk of being evicted.

I didn't quite understand why they were shunning me when I was in desperate need of help. I wasn't crazy. I wasn't mean. I wasn't trying to hurt anyone. I still believe that with some help from my family, I might have been okay. That was something I didn't ever get.

What hurts most is the fact that when I was desperate and needed help, they wouldn't talk to me. But if I seemed to be doing okay, then they'd show up. And they would only offer what they wanted to give, not necessarily what I needed. It was very limited and one-sided. Either they didn't know how to help me, or they just didn't care. I've never really known.

I remember my last night in the ward. Two fights broke out and a table broke along with some glass, and I was freaked out. There were more attacks on the nurses, and at one point this lady just looked me in the eyes and she was saying how crazy it was and how stupid it all was, and I told her to shut up. I got reprimanded for that and had to go back to my room. It was clear to me that I did not belong there. I could look around and see what was happening, without taking part in it. I asked for a meeting with a counselor to talk about that incident and to explain that I wasn't crazy; I just needed a little help. I felt completely let down, scared, and lost. If you have a family, you shouldn't be left in the state's hands, but that's what happened.

I kept telling anyone who would listen that I wanted to go home to my fiancée, go home to my dog, just go home and figure things out. My fiancée did come the next day, and she signed papers saying that she would be responsible for my well-being. She took me back to my apartment, but it was weirdly empty like someone had come in and taken my stuff while I was gone.

As it turned out, my fiancée had started packing up my things because she knew that this was the last month of my lease. I wanted to move in with her, but it wouldn't work out because she lived with a bunch of other family members, and I had a dog. So, I had to beg my mother and brother to take me back into their home, which they finally did.

It was a tough time. I thought we could work things out and move forward as a family. But things were never right between us after the shooting and my father's suicide…really after my father's cheating and the divorce. That's just the way it was. Being in the hospital and knowing that they were going to leave me there made me feel very alone and rejected.

There I was, living with people who didn't seem to care

about me. The people who were supposed to love me most. I really didn't realize how much my fiancée had done for me. She took care of my dog, she took care of my apartment, she started packing things up knowing it was my last month there, she paid my bills, she made sure I had food when I got home, and she was there for me when I needed a ride home, and later when I needed a ride to the doctor's. She was there and I didn't give her much credit, and I should have.

I hope what I've written in this chapter will give her some closure on how grateful I was. I was not ungrateful; I just didn't know how to accept the help because I had never really had a lot of help in my life before her. She saved my life. She saved my dog's life. She saved my stuff, and she saved as much as she could. I respect her and am so grateful for her.

Being put in a psych ward is tough enough, and then you see that there are people out there suffering more than you are; or maybe just differently than you are, because who can really measure anybody's problems on a scale? But the truth is that it's hard to see that there are people that are just left behind by their families, people sitting in there for years with never a visit and then we wonder why they don't get better. There's no one right way because each person is different, but we all need love and support from the people closest to us.

One of the moments that really hit me was seeing two men fight over nothing except the fact that they both wanted to feel like the guy in charge. Healthcare for mental illness is just a band-aid solution. The real work comes with the right medication, with a good counselor, and within us. Don't let people you care about suffer by themselves. Show up. Be there for them. Or at the very least, don't let someone you know who is having a hard time get to the point where they feel that they have no other option than to turn themselves in or kill themselves. I know that I have only been able to overcome my difficult times with the help of some very caring people. They're out there, you just have to find them.

Jeremy

In the months after I left my job at Starbucks, I was at this in-between point in my life. I was in my 20s but wasn't quite sure what I wanted to do. All I knew was that I wanted out of my hometown and to broaden my horizons. I took a couple months to think about where I wanted to go, what I wanted to do, and when.

I knew that a service industry job was not for me. Working retail was not for me. Even though I was good at it, I couldn't handle dealing with the public or being near so many people, at least not for long periods of time. I like to take care of people, heal them, and help in any way I can. I also knew that I enjoyed working with children and older people.

One day someone suggested that I check out a website called eNanny Source. I made a profile just to see where things could go. I passed all the background checks and was approved. Twenty minutes after signing on, I got messages from several people. One was in North Carolina and one in Texas.

All the families were interested in hiring me, and they all needed immediate help, which was perfect for me because I'm not good at sitting around and waiting. I wanted to pack up and go. Ultimately, I changed my mind about the North Carolina and Texas jobs and picked a job in Florida. The reason for choosing Florida was because the child was five years old, and he was autistic; I have a passion to help children with disabilities to find their abilities inside the disability and help them to know their triggers and grow into adults who are fully functional and confident. I also found out that the mother had a lot of heart and other health problems, so I would be helping her out as well. I knew that the father was a respected lawyer and very good at his job and very busy.

After an hour and a half on the phone talking, they got me a ticket to Treasure Island, Florida. I was in shock that I was leaving that same day on my new adventure, leaving my friends, my family and most of my belongings behind. All I had was a suitcase and my backpack.

I wasn't looking forward to the seven-hour flight as I'd never flown by myself before. I hate airports. I have a fear of losing track of the kids I'm watching or being late for my plane and missing my flight and having to sleep on the floor of the airport.

As I got off the phone, I was still in shock. I couldn't believe I was leaving in a mere four hours. I went inside and packed. I told my mother, and she took me to the airport, no questions asked. I was nervous, tired, and excited. I have never picked up my life like that and moved away so fast and so freely with nothing really holding me back.

After getting to the airport and getting my ticket, saying goodbye to my mother, I was off. I went up the stairwell to the terminals for the first time as an adult on my own. As I was waiting for my plane, I was doing some reading on the family and found out that they were very successful and very well known throughout the community and the state. I read all the information I could on the plane about the family. When we landed, I went down and got my luggage and went outside. I had to smoke a cigarette quickly because I did not tell them I smoked. I was waiting outside the airport in Florida, and I had never experienced humidity like that before in my life. I was sweating like crazy.

As the van pulled up, the mother got out and gave me a hug. Her sister was driving because the mother couldn't drive due to seizures and other health issues. As we pulled away from Tampa International Airport, I was in awe at the beauty of Treasure Island. I was also in shock when the sister and the mom lit up cigarettes in the car. I was really relieved. As we drove to the house in Treasure Island, we talked a lot about expectations and how the job would go, and a lot about Jeremy, the five-year-old who was struggling with school.

Their home was stunning. It was an expansive three-story house with a pool underneath, sitting right on the Gulf of Mexico. We walked in and here comes this little adorable little kid charging down the stairs. He looked at me and he said my name and he shook my hand. I was really impressed with his manners.

As we walked upstairs, I met the husband, Simon, who was short and stocky with a firm handshake. He thanked me for coming on such short notice and asked me if I was ready to start work. I said yes. We all went upstairs, and they showed me my room. My plane came in at midnight Florida time so I was exhausted. I was in for a surprise the next morning, though, as we were all going to go to Disney World for Jeremy's birthday. I had never been and was excited about it. I was also nervous because I'd just gotten there and didn't know anything or anyone. Disney World was loud and overwhelming, but I had a wonderful time anyway. Just watching how much fun Jeremy had was a real treat.

As soon as we got back to our regular days, the work really started. The household got up at 6:00 a.m. and we would go upstairs and get our coffee and drink it, overlooking the Gulf of Mexico and Boca Ciega Bay. It was a gorgeous start for my first real day.

At 7:00 a.m. sharp every day, we would get Jeremy up. He had three things for breakfast, either peanut butter and jelly, homemade macaroni and cheese, or eggs with ketchup and toast with butter and cinnamon sugar. He would eat nothing else, and he'd only drink chocolate milk.

Some days we had medical appointments, which were usually early so we would get up earlier than normal. We would always eat at the hospital and Jeremy would always get chocolate chip pancakes.

When I would wake up Jeremy in the morning, I had to have his chocolate milk ready to go; he would not get out of bed without that in a sippy cup. As he would roll around moaning, groaning, and complaining about getting up to go to school, I would iron and starch his uniform and then lay it on his bed. And then after breakfast he would say goodbye to his dad, who he would only see for 20 minutes in the morning. He would then go to the shower, and just sit in there. At times trying to stay in there for almost an hour so that we had to rush him to get himself dressed. He would sometimes help me make his bed and then we would go to the living room, and he would be able to watch cartoons for a half hour. After that, he would usually run downstairs and get in the van.

I would then take him to school and when it was just the two of us, it was very different from being with his parents, which is typical with all kids...but he was very intrigued with where I came from, where I wanted to go in life, and what I was doing in Florida. We would have very adult conversations on the way to school. I would park the car and walk him to the door. Jeremy would always promise me with a handshake that he would have a good day at school.

After I dropped him off, I would usually stop at the store to pick up two packs of cigarettes for Simon and anything the house needed before I headed home. You would think that's when the day would kind of slow down. But no, that's when it just got started. They had a 4,500 square-foot home with six bedrooms and four baths. It was part of my job to help clean it. I was going full bore. I'd make all the beds; then clean the bathrooms and they were very meticulous about how they wanted it done and I followed the standards as best as I could.

There were Sundays where I would go lay on the bed in the spare room and just fall asleep. I would be so tired because at times, Jeremy wouldn't sleep at night because of his manic mode, and I had to care for him.

After cleaning the house and eating lunch, I would go pick Jeremy up and he would show me his daily report. School was challenging for Jeremy so there were more bad days than good ones, but if he got a good report, he earned a small reward. We would pick him up and he would always ask for a toy and usually he got it even if I disagreed, but I wasn't the parent.

At this point in Jeremy's life, he would throw fits, throw things at his mom, and try to push her down the stairs. He would take pots and pans and throw them. He would throw books. He would break things. He would get angry and just fly off the handle.

The techniques his parents had been using were simply not working so I had to figure how to help him handle his emotions better. They would constantly yell at him and tell him what he was doing wrong. Growing up on the autism spectrum myself, I knew that doesn't work for me and it definitely didn't work for him.

So, I decided to talk to the doctor about ways and solutions. The doctor made some changes to some of his medication, and we started going out for walks and getting him more exercise. The previous nanny rarely took him out for exercise, and he would come home and just watch TV. I cut that out of our routine and took him down to the park when he got home, or we went swimming in the house's pool or next-door at the resort, or we just went shopping.

It was all kind of left up to me as I was the full-time nanny. I worked hard to help Jeremy self-regulate his outbursts and probably the most important thing I did for him was to insist on helping him become a good swimmer. This became an outlet for both of us, and it was amazing to have the ocean at our doorstep. I lasted seven years at that job, which remains my all-time record. And from what I've heard, Jeremy has turned into a successful, productive adult and a really decent human being.

Football Drinking Drama

It was a Thursday afternoon in Treasure Island, Florida. I was anticipating the arrival of my second set of 'parents' to fly in from Oregon. We had grown close when I fostered their grandchildren. I had always called them Mom and Dad. I had unconsciously searched for a replacement family after I'd grown estranged from my own family after the shooting and my dad's suicide. They were arriving at Tampa International Airport. I was so excited as it had been at least a year since I'd last seen them. I was so looking forward to having them meet the boy I cared for, Jeremy, and his family. Jeremy had heard a lot about them, so he was excited to meet them as well.

That night, we were all getting done with dinner and my mom went downstairs to get the bags. When she came up from downstairs, I saw that she had a suitcase full of New Orleans Saints sportswear. Jeremy was so excited when Mom pulled out a New Orleans Saints original jersey. Jeremy had never been involved in watching sports with his focus being mainly on Legos, and computers.

We were going to the football game the next day and now Jeremy had a cool jersey to wear. Someone that Dad knew had gotten us sideline passes before the game and got us great seats behind the Saints field goal, which was thrilling.

Jeremy, mom, dad, and I were decked out in Saints colors—black and gold—and surrounded by Tampa Bay fans. The fans were actually quite nice to us and welcomed us throughout the morning, as we walked over to the media line. With being able to pass through the lines at the stadium, Jeremy and I (both of us on the autism spectrum) were doing well by avoiding all the drunken tailgaters, and the loud, die-hard NFL fans. We got through the media lines and were allowed to enter onto the field when the Saints came out for pre-game practice. At the end of the practice, we were then walked over to the bleachers and escorted from the field to our seats.

We were enjoying the game, but the crowd was really loud and pretty vocally brutal as the game went on. Everyone was drinking a lot and the volume kept going up with every beer. I knew it was all in fun, but it was a lot. When the second quarter hit, I took several pain pills thinking that since I am not a drinker, they might soften the edges a bit and make it easier to enjoy the festive atmosphere.

This was a mistake. But everyone else was drinking around me and I just wanted to take part in the fun. Or maybe I just wanted to calm myself down. I'm not sure which. Being in a crowd that large was not easy for me, as someone on the spectrum and as a survivor of trauma.

As we got closer to halftime, the score was about even, and

we could see, off in the very near distance, the squall line of rain heading our way. As halftime started, the thunderstorms hit, and they had everyone from the stadium and field file inside the halls in order to ensure our safety. However, as the hallways filled up with all the fans, my head started to go dark. The thoughts of us being struck by lightning or someone opening fire on the crowds started to flood my mind. It was my PTSD rearing its ugly head. I ordered a beer from the vendor's stall. My 'parents' were there so I knew that Jeremy was safe, and I could let loose a bit, which is something I never, ever do. As I said, I am not a drinker, so, this was my second mistake.

I continued to let my fear run wild in my head and as I did, the alcohol that I was drinking did make everything worse. I finally felt the Vicodin kick in to its full effect and my mind and body were pretty much out of control. I barely remember the second half of the game starting or going back out to our seats. It was a blackout moment. Apparently, I started using vulgar words and was getting pretty hostile with nearby fans.

I honestly don't remember a thing. I do remember needing help to get down the stairs and throwing up on the people below us. We had to leave the stadium because of me. I also remember that the car ride home was a horrible experience for Jeremy because my 'parents' were yelling at me, and Jeremy had never seen someone blackout drunk before.

When we arrived home, I realized that I couldn't get out of the car. Jeremy was yelling at me, telling me that I ruined everything, and I just remember laying down in the middle of the driveway puking my brains out. As I lay there in a stupor, everyone else went upstairs to finish watching the rest of the game, which the Saints came back and won. The continued drama on the driveway made my 'parents' resent me even more, since they had flown a long way to give us the gift of a day of football. All because I could not handle being huddled in that hallway. The similarity to another space I was once huddled in was just too much for me.

I am not proud of how I dealt with the situation, but I simply didn't have the tools to handle it better. I can honestly say that I have not had one drink since that day, nor have I taken a pill for non-medicinal purposes. I guess I had to really embarrass myself and feel that shame, in order to learn my limits. But what I also learned is that PTSD can hit me at any time, and I now make a conscious effort to avoid situations which might trigger it or remove myself early. If I hear fireworks or a gun shot, or if I'm in a crowd or an enclosed space where I might get trapped, I still feel that familiar panic, but I can get through it without the use of any substances, which is a step in the right direction.

Los Angeles

I moved in with this girl named Lisa in downtown Los Angeles off of Melrose Boulevard on Vista Drive. It was a packed house. It was a one-bedroom apartment with Lisa, two dogs, me, and another guy. I used to walk up and down Melrose just checking out the shops and the clothing items and the history of it all. But more significantly, it was also my first time experiencing the gay scene with rainbow crosswalks and seeing guys holding hands, girls holding hands, all of them being totally accepted. It was a mind shocker to me.

I know Oregon is considered a liberal state, but that's mostly Portland and Eugene. My hometown of Springfield wasn't like that. I remember walking past this jewelry store in L.A. where a guy was standing outside. I stopped and spoke with him, asked for a cigarette, and then I went inside to look at some jewelry and he was telling me how he needed help around that place because it was just too much for him working there 12-14 hours a day.

I offered to work for him, and he hired me on the spot. Gave me a nice necklace right off the bat and a watch, as part of a signing bonus to start working. This old guy, he was quite a character—really goofy, smart as hell, and connected all over L.A. He had been a Hollywood producer years ago, and he still knew people.

Monday after work, he asked me to go to this lady's house with him. Although she lived just a few short blocks from the store, we got into his car because everyone drives everywhere in L.A. As we walked in the door, I saw this gorgeous, absolutely stunning woman: 6'2", blonde hair and a smile that would light up any room. Confidence like no other and then a kiwi accent from New Zealand comes out. She seemed worldly and sophisticated. And I embraced it. She came over and she air-kissed my boss and then me cheek-to-cheek and introduced herself as Jayne.

We all sat down, and we talked about an event that she was going to have at her club in downtown L.A. She was a part owner of this club, and she was holding a charity event including the remaining members of The Temptations and several old bands, and a few new bands as well.

Soon after this, I was offered a job as a personal assistant to this incredible woman. Included as perks with the position were so many wonderful things: I got to hear so many stories, I got to learn about interior design, I got to learn about running a night club, and working with talent. I came to profoundly respect this lady who came from nothing. I am so grateful for that time. It really felt like my luck was changing, and that I had landed the job of a lifetime...all I had to do was keep it together.

Alcoholics Anonymous

I was 28 when I started going to Alcoholics Anonymous with a friend of mine while I was working for her jewelry company in West Hills, California. Ellie asked me to support her by going with her to a meeting, so I did. As I was sitting there, I related a lot to what they were talking about, even though I did not have a problem with alcohol.

I can't say that I was 100% clean and sober at that time in my life, but I wasn't a big substance abuser, and I didn't drink. Upon arrival, everyone was so kind and nice. Ellie shared her story, which was very moving and hit home with a lot of what I was going through. She introduced me to a couple more people, and I found myself going back to AA meetings consistently. I could see that this was a kind of support system that was really worth sticking with.

After my first 30 days, I found myself getting to speak a lot, even at ten-minute meetings. As my trauma story got out, I found myself being asked more and more to speak and then it was almost turning into an hour-long speech. It is difficult for me to speak at public events, or even with a close group of friends. But since I was speaking my truth, I found it to be easier because I knew that these people would relate and they were not there to judge, but rather to listen and be a part of my journey.

As time went on, I needed to move out of Ellie's house and into my own place. There was a regular named Jenny at the meetings, and she and I always chatted before and after. She had known some very dark times and knew how to be a helping hand that you need at times in life. She had a place off of Oxnard Blvd., and I stayed there a couple nights. When my employment changed and I started working at Nordstrom, she offered to let me move in with her. Things were pretty great; we had some really good times.

I worked five days a week and attended all my AA meetings. I was busy, and I enjoyed life at that point, even with no car and having to use the bus line to get around town. After hitting a year of substance sobriety, speaking at over 45 meetings and being a sponsor and finishing my 12 Steps, I was really proud of myself. I felt like I'd accomplished something real. I remember taking my one-year birthday cake and standing up there on stage being so proud that I had hit the year milestone. I took my cake at every meeting for a week straight and was proud every time I got up on that stage and got that one-year chip.

It was after the one-year AA meeting, and after a week of taking my one-year cakes at all my meetings, that I finally decided to test the waters again, thinking that I was strong enough to keep going without AA. But I soon ran into this guy who I'll call James. He was very handsome and had a nice place, and was also exactly the guy I shouldn't, but wanted to, have. He was a good man, but deeply troubled. I met his family and all his friends, and everything seemed great. However, one day I found him shooting up ketamine which is an animal tranquilizer, so I tried it with him, and I found myself craving it days later and finally I broke down. I went into a deep, dark abyss and my whole time at AA and all my friends and family sort of went down the drain.

I am still, to this day, sad about my decision to give up on myself and all I had achieved just for a man and a drug. James did me very wrong soon after this. I guess you could say that I learned my lesson the hard way, and I knew right away that substance abuse was not going to be a part of who I was, going forward. I am forever grateful that I can look back on the experience of AA and take away something really good from it.

James

After Jayne, the former Playboy Bunny/interior designer/ club owner, hired me as her Personal Assistant, I had to find a place to live. I bounced around from couch to couch. Then I met someone. A man. Since I hadn't been out when I was younger, James and his group had me under their spell. However, the relationship with James quickly turned to one of callous abuse and domination. Yes, there were drugs involved. I even took part in AA and NA meetings in the area, where I met a number of celebrities who were struggling with addictions.

My living situation was less than ideal but I felt helpless to get out of it. I was living in a new city, with a new job, just trying to make something of myself and maybe meet some people and have some fun, and I needed a place to live. I am a tall guy and I consider myself to be of strong spirit but fighting or any kind of physical violence are painful and traumatic for me. Because of this, I tend to get pushed around a lot. So, this story is a difficult one to tell.

Things with James sunk to their lowest level one night when he and his friends got a hold of some Ketamine, and they injected it into me until I was passed out. I woke up later to something going on which I cannot even bring myself to describe. It is the most heinous act of taking advantage of someone when they are unconscious, but they did it. They gang-raped me. Though I somehow survived this incident, the abuse from James continued to the point where he severely beat me up and I managed to get myself, bloody and exhausted, to the Los Angeles airport where I called my family to see if they would buy me a ticket home to Oregon. They refused. I was desperate and had no idea what to do until an airport employee took pity on me and bought me a one-way ticket back to Oregon.

To say that this has changed the way I relate to people physically is accurate, but an understatement. I don't like to be touched, or hugged, but I do my best to be my kind and generous self, so I don't shun contact with other humans completely. It is just hard sometimes, to always have to draw the line and keep a protective shell around myself.

Martin

Martin was 38 when I met him. About 5'4" with a shaved head and beautiful light brown skin with a reddish undertone. His voice was confident with a hint of vulnerability. He was a man of wisdom and strength and immense patience. Martin was willing to teach as long as you were able to really listen and would try to apply those lessons to your life. I've never felt so intrigued by someone; this man taught me many lessons of the Earth and a way to live without working harder but instead, working smarter. I want to share our journey, and I'm proud to call him my Jedi Master.

During my time with Martin, I learned not only to love myself but to love others in a way I never have before. I met Martin through my friend Terry, who was my foster son's swim coach.

My respect for Martin is deep. Martin first started coming to the house where Terry and I lived to help us grow our first batch of marijuana. Martin taught me how to measure and cut wood correctly in addition to teaching me all the basics of growing marijuana, as it was becoming legal to grow it and sell it in the state we were in. Martin came over every other day and taught me how to keep everything on the up and up, and we became close.

At around the same time, Terry's and my friendship was coming to an end. Terry and I were fighting more and more because we'd become too close and things got a bit awkward and uncomfortable. The fighting and yelling turned to walkouts and blowouts. One time, Terry walked out on me around Christmas time and it was in the middle of a grow cycle of plants. We both decided that we could not live together any longer, but we wanted to remain friends and also finish out this cycle of growing weed.

Martin had invested in us as well, and we could not just cut everything and be done. Martin continued to show up and he taught me so much. It was coming to the end of the growing, and I finally became really vulnerable thinking I would get cast out.

One day, Martin and I sat down at the table and he asked me what my plans were since I had no money, no job, and only a car and a dog. I turned to Martin and started to cry and told him that I didn't know what I was going to do. I asked him with tears flooding my eyes to allow me to work for him and to stay in this house and grow. Like the great man he is, Martin said yes and continued to pay all the bills and allowed me to stay in my house for two more months.

One day, we found black mold in the bathroom. That black mold turned out to be a nightmare. The whole bathroom had to be ripped out. The floor, the sink, the tub, and the toilet. It became uninhabitable. I started staying at a neighbor's house for a short period of time before we decided it was time to close shop and move forward. So I went from living there to living in my car and then temporarily staying with Martin at his house out in the country. The only problem was that his Akita and my Black Lab did not get along at all. It caused a lot of problems to the point where my dog was restricted to my car and half of the grow room. Eventually, I started sleeping in one of the bedrooms and my dog was allowed in with me. I continued to work with Martin, and it began to really feel like home. I benefited from having a place to live and Martin benefited from having a hard-working young man who was respectful and willing to learn and accept his knowledge and his lead.

Martin continued to work with me and encouraged me to go back to school and to set my sights higher than I ever thought was possible. Martin took me to a concert of this local band that had just formed called Fortune's Folly. We went to one show, and it was amazing. I have never felt so alive as I did then. From that moment on, we were Fortune's Folly fans. I worked with Martin for the next six months.

Martin taught me to believe in manifesting, and getting things done by working smarter not harder. He taught me how to nourish our bodies and to take care of them instead of poisoning ourselves and feeling worse. I learned how to play golf, and to enjoy life again after years of misery. You might say that Martin was a kind of savior to me, in addition to being a mentor. I am a very confident man in the world today. I am happy and confident (even though my confidence is sometimes mistaken for cockiness). A lot of that is because of Martin and his kindness to me.

I finally took off after six months of living with Martin, to take his lessons and knowledge and decided to go "fly on my own." I moved to Vancouver, Washington, and made it for about three months before the world came crashing back in and I tried to commit suicide. I ended up overdosing and Martin somehow got me home to his place, although I do not quite remember how. All I know is that Martin had rescued me once again. I remember coming home and being surprised by so many of our friends.

We sat by the fire all night, cuddled up and surrounded by so many good people. Martin pulled out all the stops for me to make sure I felt loved. We even had an acoustic concert by Fortune's Folly. They played by the fire while we listened to them sing. It was great. I worked for Martin for a few more weeks, and then I finally landed a job nearby, taking care of an elderly man. I got the new job, and I moved in that day.

I would like to sincerely thank Martin for all the knowledge and life-lessons he taught me, and for quite literally saving my life. I will forever be grateful and will continue to move forward in my life in honor of our time together.

Chapter K

I first met this girl named K at Terry's house. Terry was my foster kid Justin's swim coach. She came walking downstairs wearing white shorts and a turquoise top with dangling earrings that brushed the top of her shoulders. Her smile gleamed ear to ear and her energy was on fire. She shook my hand, and I felt at that moment in time that I had found a new friend who would be really special to me. Little did I know, I'd find a life-long friend and one that made the biggest impression to date on my life. It was actually June 1, 2013, around 4 p.m. We sat around and chatted about life—mainly Justin and Terry—and had a few drinks and then she took off. I knew at that point that she was a good person.

It was several days before she came around again. There was the same feeling as before...like we had been friends forever. Her energy was great, and she had nothing but positive things to say. We went on to have a perfect night. I remember her asking about my past and as always getting my emotions wrapped up into that. She was a bit younger than I was, but she was wise beyond her years. She had a spiritual side to her which was something I hadn't encountered in too many other people.

A week later, Terry and I decided to get a house together. He and I secured the house and moved right in. My job was to clean up, organize, take care of the yard, and watch and grow our marijuana crop. Terry had to go on a three-week trip, first with his swim team and then a raft trip with his family. Over those three weeks, K agreed to stay with me due to the fact that I did not enjoy staying home alone in a new place by myself. I was still having nightmares and panic attacks about the past. Even though I felt safe, it was nice knowing that someone would be there to run to or to yell for or to somehow pull me out of it…or just someone to be there in the mornings.

During our first night together, she encountered me having the night terrors, the waking up abruptly, the crying, and the terror in my eyes upon wakening. It was a realization for her to the fact that I was definitely traumatized, and it was not made up or fake, or blown out of proportion. As our days went on, our conversations got deeper and deeper. The way she asked questions, I felt so safe. It felt like it was okay to really answer for the first time in my life.

She showed no judgement, said nothing back, just provided an ear, and a whole bunch of compassion and love. We would sit at the dining room table in the house talking for hours, getting lost in conversation, and nothing else and no one else mattered. It started to take shape that she was about to help me free myself of some of my trauma and help me day by day to be a better man, not only for myself but to everyone around me and out in the world.

Through the years, K has made such an impression on my life. She has helped me express how grateful I am for people in my life and how sorry I am for harsh things I might have said. As a kid, I knew that my mom and dad loved me, but the divorce, the shooting, and the suicide left our family broken and destroyed.

I don't know if I had ever experienced true unconditional love before K, but it is definitely the biggest lesson I learned from her: That, and how we can manifest everything we do and have.

Nido

I got my dog Nido off Craigslist in May 2014. At first, I got him as a guard dog to watch the house. It was the first time I had a big yard, and a place of my own to have a dog in. When I saw Nido on Craigslist he was a one-year-old. He was raised by a nine-year-old boy, and they were getting ready to move somewhere where they could not have the dog. I saw the ad, and I immediately knew that I was going to take him. I got on the phone and made a call to the veterinarian and told him that I have a dog and I need to bring him in. I made the appointment for the same day, and that is when I knew I was going to be a dog dad.

When Nido's previous family finally arrived at my front door, I was so excited. They opened the car door, and he came out and was running like crazy all over the yard—running and just going nuts. The owners came out of the car and said "Here's Nido!" and I said, "I'll take him." I also told them that they could follow me on Facebook, and I would update them with Nido's progress.

Nido came into the house and raised hell, chewing everything, running all over the house like he'd been kept in a room for months. He was raised by a nine-year-old boy for the last year and had no manners. No discipline, nothing. We went to the veterinarian and Nido had his first check-up. While he was in the vet getting his test done, I went next door and spent $200 on toys, blankets and food.

I took Nido home, and we had a great night. It was the first night of a long-term commitment, but I was not exactly sure how it was going to go.

The next morning, I had plans to go to my aunt's house to watch the Saints play and I was not going to take him over there, so I left him at the house. When I came back from the Saints game, my house was destroyed. The curtains were taken off the walls. My bed was chewed up. The kitchen towels were chewed up. He had peed everywhere. It was awful. I didn't know at that point if I would be able to keep him.

Then one day, I was outside playing in the yard with him, and he made friends with the neighbor's dog. The owner came and said "Hey, let's introduce the dogs." The neighbor and I started talking, and we realized that we had a lot of stuff in common as I suffer from PTSD and so did she. She was a dog trainer for veterans with PTSD and she offered to help me train my dog and opened up my eyes to the whole world of service dogs. She said that Nido would be able to go anywhere with me, to be there for me full time. He'd learn how to help cope with my daily struggles and to be able to be the dog that I'd always dreamed of.

Nido's training began that day and he learned all the basics quickly: how to sit, shake, lie down, etc. Eventually Nido would be the one to help me cope with my nightmares. I have had nightmares and night terrors ever since the shooting, but I never knew how to cope with them. It wasn't until I saw Nido in action that it all came together. That evening, I started having a nightmare and Nido, without me realizing it, woke me up as the nightmare started. I tend to be a sound sleeper, but he would pounce on me. He would jump on me. He'd do anything he could to get me to wake up when a nightmare started to occur. That is when I knew I had the exact right dog. No question.

As Nido and I began our journey together, I had no idea what an amazing impact this dog would have on my life. He became my everything. Would he go to the store with me? Would he sleep in the bed with me? He would be there for me without even asking. I started taking oats to this horse to see how Nido would react in the presence of another animal, and he did great. I started taking him in public with me and making appearances. He became more confident in himself and in us and with his confidence, came my own.

Nido has been an essential part of my daily life, and I don't know what I would do without him or what I'm going to do once he's not around. I can't even think about it. It puts me into a state of shock to even think about it. Nido has been such a gift to me and the community around me. He's so gentle and attentive with older people and children who want to pet him.

He's just a really good dog.

I've only been separated from Nido two times for more than a day. The first time was when he was neutered, and it was horrible. I cried my eyes out because they wanted me to leave him there on the table in the cage and I said no. I said you can put him to sleep and then I will leave. When I left him, I went and bought him everything you could dream of. I bought him a new bed, blankets, toys. Everything I could find. When I went to go pick him up from the vet, I was crying my eyes out and they told me that he had to walk out of the vet in order for them to release him and I just picked him up and started walking out and left. I went home and I put my house on lockdown: no one was coming over until Nido was fully healed. I wasn't completely rational about it.

The last time I left him was when he tore his ACLs in both his back legs, and that nearly killed me because my dog, till this day, is still not the same. I'm no longer able to 'work' him. I'm not able to take him with me to most of the places I used to bring him. I have learned how to cope with my anxiety in different ways and I have made the adjustments needed to take care of Nido's legs as they are now. I hate leaving him at home. I hate seeing him not run, but I'm so grateful that he's still alive.

Nido is getting older and with his surgeries he has changed a little bit, and our whole lives have changed. He's a little bit grumpier. But that's okay. Aren't we all? He still sleeps up on the bed. He still wakes me up in a minute. Still provides that care. He never leaves my side, and he still is the key essential to me living somewhat of a normal life. Whatever that is. Nido has changed my life in so many ways, I will always love and care for him. Nido has made everybody's day a little bit brighter no matter how long or how little time you get to spend with him.

We now live in the Southwest. He loves the heat, and he loves to be outdoors. But most of all, he likes to be next to me and that unconditional love is something that no one, and I mean no one, can ever provide me or will ever provide me the way he has. He has saved my life. He saved me from suicide attempts over and over again. No matter where we were, how much we were struggling, that dog has always been one of my guardian angels.

'Dad'

This is the story of an elderly man with dementia issues. He had no sense of real time, what day it was, where his wife was, what had happened recently. He was just stuck in a rest home waiting, while his family was expecting him to die. This is a story of courage and hope. I had just moved out of a house in Eugene, and I'd ended up suing my landlord for mold in the bathroom. Didn't get much money from it, but I left there more knowledgeable and more confident than ever before. It was a transition between homes, and I was staying with friends, but I was mostly staying with my friend Martin.

One morning in May, I decided to stop at Spencer Butte and take the Ridgeline Trail. If you've never been to Oregon, it was one of those spring mornings where it was crisp and cold but absolutely gorgeous. I decided to go on Craigslist and look at ads for caregivers; I don't know why. I had nothing better to do and it was too nice out to go back to my car and go home so I decided to stick it out and I found this caregiving ad that said, 'A man looking for in-home care.' I replied to the message and got a phone call 15 minutes later. I answered the phone, and it was a lady from Elder Care Resources, a company that was hired to work with Donald, to get him help and to manage it.

We made an appointment for that afternoon for me to meet her at the rehabilitation place, where I would meet Donald and his brother and see what we could do. I wasn't expecting anything out of it. I told them up front that I had a service dog, and she was okay with that, and she said it would be up to the family and Donald if it would work for them. If it wasn't, then I simply wouldn't take the job.

As I was approaching the rest home, I was quite nervous. I pulled into the rest home parking lot, I went to the front desk and there was a lady there who greeted me and showed me to the cafeteria, where I met the lady from Elder Care and Donald's brother, Gerald.

We sat around and chatted for a little bit and then Donald approached us in a wheelchair without any emotion on his face. He sat down there with us and apparently, for the first time in weeks, he made a slight sign of progress, smiling at my dog, Nido. He then looked up at me and put his hands out and asked me if he could pet my dog and I said, "Absolutely."

At this point Donald's brother and the lady from Elder Care gave us about 20 minutes alone to talk. It was mainly me talking, but he did contribute. And he obviously loved Nido as he kept petting him the whole time.

I asked Donald if he wanted to go home, and he said he'd been wanting to go home for a very long time. By the time his brother and the other lady came back, we had already decided he was going home, and I was going to take the job. When they came back to the table, that's how it went, and when they asked me if I wanted to accept the position I said, "Yes, absolutely."

I was directed to go with Gerald and get Donald's belongings and meet everyone out front. After months of Donald being practically unresponsive other than asking to escape, he became totally engaged in what was going on. His brother gave me the address to his house, and I met Donald and his brother there. It was a gorgeous house in the woods, a beautiful A-frame with a huge front and backyard, a large Koi pond…it was absolutely stunning.

He also had a huge woodworking shop which was, strangely, all packed up and Donald didn't understand why his house was all packed up. We walked in the front door, and everything was pretty much packed up the way you do when you're moving out. He had a dog named Jason, a tall Doberman; a beautiful brown dog who was so excited to see his dad, and Donald was very excited to see him.

Donald then let Nido come in and Nido and Jason ran around like crazy and enjoyed playing together. Donald and Gerald and I sat down and just went over some basic things like his physical condition, the house, the address, his contact info--all the necessities. Gerald told me he would be back in two days, and we would talk some more.

In the meantime, I had just gotten started with getting Donald settled into his house and suddenly Gerald pulled me outside to tell me that Donald's wife passed away while he was in the hospital, and I guess I was supposed to tell him. Broke my heart. Apparently, she fell asleep while driving to see him and crashed her car on the way to the hospital. Back inside, I told Donald about it, and he was a bit shocked. But then he said he kind of knew that she must have passed because she was not visiting him every day like she used to.

And then he said that his family basically ignored him and just left him there. He said he didn't have much love for his brother, or any other member of his family and he pretty much wanted to just come home and die, but I decided I wasn't about to let that happen.

I fixed dinner for the two of us, then got Donald settled in bed, and then took both the dogs out to go to the bathroom. After that I got the dishes cleaned up and I just went to my room, and I sat there; I wasn't sure if I was supposed to sleep near him or just stay awake and listen for him to see if he might fall down the stairs. I was completely worried, so I went and slept at the bottom of the stairs to make sure he was safe.

Somehow, I felt immediately protective of this old guy. Of course, in the middle of the night I saw him trying to get up and go downstairs, so I stopped him and when he told me that he was trying to get something to eat or drink, I grabbed a pudding for each of us, went upstairs and gave him a Coke and we sat out on his balcony and talked. That conversation on the balcony that night is one that I will never forget. It was heavy. It was emotional.

I worked for him for the next two years, doing regular physical therapy with him and helping his general health to improve. I came to think of him as my 'dad,' and I really felt he thought of me as a son. He eventually passed away, leaving me with another dad-sized hole in my heart. Perhaps the experience taught me to maintain more of a professional distance and not become quite so attached to the people in my care. Lesson learned.

Thanks, Dad. Rest in Peace

About the Author

Noah Nash was raised in Springfield, Oregon, and is one of the surviviors of the Thurston High School shooting in 1998. His life was indelibly altered by that event and the suicide of his father. In this collection of essays, Nash provides us with a glimpse of his journey, with all its twists and turns, hoping to show readers that he has survived, in spite of being neurodivergent and experiencing a double-dose of trauma at a young age.

By developing street-smarts and leaning on various people Nash met along the way, he remained dedicated to finding work and making the most of himself, even when things did not go to plan. His is a story of what can happen to someone who needs help but tends to slip through the cracks. There are many such people who surround us but do not have the voice to share their trials and tribulations, leaving them alienated and in the shadows. While attempting to speak up for this silent minority, Nash also wants readers to know that he is simply trying to do his best.

Milton Keynes UK
Ingram Content Group UK Ltd.
UKHW011434140724
445326UK00004B/182